Designed by Eddie Goldfine
Layout by Ariane Rybski
Edited by Sorelle Weinstein
Photography by Danya Weiner
Culinary Editing by Tamar Zakut
Nutritional Information by Rachel Granot, B.Sc., M.P.H.

STERLING and the distinctive Sterling logo are registered trademarks of
Sterling Publishing Co., Inc.

Library of Congress Cataloging-in-Publication Data

Laskin, Avner.
Honey : more than 75 delicious recipes / Avner Laskin ; photography by Danya Weiner.
p. cm.
Includes index.
ISBN 978-1-4027-4936-0
1. Cookery (Honey) I. Title.
TX767.H7L37 2008
641.3'8--dc22   2008010205

10 9 8 7 6 5 4 3 2 1

Published by Sterling Publishing Co., Inc.
387 Park Avenue South, New York, NY 10016
© 2008 by Penn Publishing Ltd.
Distributed in Canada by Sterling Publishing
$^c/_o$ Canadian Manda Group, 165 Dufferin Street,
Toronto, Ontario, Canada M6K 3H6
Distributed in the United Kingdom by GMC Distribution Services,
Castle Place, 166 High Street, Lewes, East Sussex, England BN7 1XU
Distributed in Australia by Capricorn Link (Australia) Pty. Ltd.
P.O. Box 704, Windsor, NSW 2756, Australia

Printed in China
All rights reserved

Sterling ISBN 978-1-4027-4936-0

For information about custom editions, special sales, premium and
corporate purchases, please contact Sterling Special Sales
Department at 800-805-5489 or specialsales@sterlingpublishing.com.

AVNER LASKIN

HONEY

More than 75 Delicious Recipes

PHOTOGRAPHY BY DANYA WEINER

STERLING

New York / London
www.sterlingpublishing.com

TABLE OF CONTENTS

DESSERTS AND DRINKS 102

INDEX 126

ALL ABOUT HONEY

"Well," said Pooh, "what I like best—" and then he had to stop and think. Because although Eating Honey was a very good thing to do, there was a moment just before you began to eat it which was better than when you were, but he didn't know what it was called. —Winnie the Pooh

Humans have been collecting honey as food for thousands of years. Ancient cave drawings depict prehistoric man gathering honeycomb and storing it in baskets. The Bible contains frequent references to honey as a symbol for all that is good and desirable. Buddhist monks celebrate the holiday of Madhu Purnima ("honey full moon"), which commemorates an episode in which a monkey brought the Buddha honey as a gift. In ancient Egypt and Rome, honey was even used as currency. In modern days, honey is used in everything from cooking and baking to cosmetics and pharmaceuticals.

Because of its versatility in cooking, honey is used in diverse and delicious recipes. Entrées and appetizers, desserts and drinks are all made better with the delicious taste of honey. In this book you will find a plethora of ways to make plain recipes superb and you will learn new recipes that showcase the rich satisfying flavor of Mother Nature's sweet golden surprise, honey.

This book contains more than 75 recipes that highlight the versatility of honey. In **Breakfast**, you will find recipes for *Honey Pancakes* (page 24) and *Cinnamon Honey Donuts* (page 32) which are great ways to start your day with honey's golden goodness. **Baked Goods** will teach you how to incorporate honey into many types of breads and savory pastries such as *Honey Cake with Caramelized Oranges* (page 36) and *Goat Cheese–Stuffed Honey Rye Loaf* (page 46).

Salads and Entrées provides wonderful ways to use honey in healthy salads and savory vegetable and meat dishes such as *Honey-Glazed Chicken Breasts* (page 74), *Crispy Calamari with Honey Sauce* (page 80), and *Chinese Noodles and Vegetables in Ginger Honey Sauce* (page 84). Of course, no cookbook about honey would be complete without a chapter on **Desserts and Drinks** which contains *White Chocolate Mousse with Honey-Glazed Almonds* (page 110) and *Saffron Honey Panna Cotta* (page 118), two of the restaurant-quality recipes which serve as a fitting end to our exploration of honey.

When following the recipes in Honey, you will notice that I have not used a specific type of honey for any recipe. I have chosen recipes which are suitable for all types of honey, and the reader may use the honey of his or her preference. Each type of honey will impart its own unique flavor to the recipes in this book. Enjoy!

Bon appetit!
Avner Laskin

WHERE HONEY COMES FROM

Honey is the sweet, viscous food which honeybees produce from the nectar of flowers. The bees gather the floral nectar and transport it in their "honey stomachs" back to the hive, where it is collected and processed by other bees. In the hive, enzymes are added to the nectar to break it down into simpler sugars and to prevent the formation of bacteria. The resulting fluid is spread out over the honeycomb, where exposure to air helps to evaporate moisture from the fluid and thicken it. Bees in the hive even fan their wings over the processed nectar to help circulate the air and decrease the drying time. The honey that results from this process is then stored and used as a food source by the bees. When beekeepers harvest honey, they artificially encourage overproduction of honey in the hive so that they may harvest the excess without endangering the bees' food supply.

TYPES OF HONEY

Several types of honey are available for home use.

Blended—A mixture of two or more honeys which are derived from different varieties of flowers and which differ in taste, color, density, and/or geographic origin.

Polyfloral—Honey which is derived from the nectar of more than one flower.

Monofloral—Honey which is derived from a single type of flower. Beekeepers ensure that the honey is purely monofloral by allowing the bees access only to a single floral type.

Honeydew—Honey made from honeydew instead of nectar. It is stronger in flavor than regular honey.

In addition to the many different varieties of honey available, honey is also sold in different forms.

Organic—Honey that is produced without using pesticides or artificial fertilizers. Can be difficult to find as beekeepers usually need to use many chemicals and additives in order to ensure healthy, usable honey.

Raw—Unprocessed honey or honey not heated above 120°F. May contain particles of beeswax and/or pollen.

Chunk—Honey sold with chunks of honeycomb.

Strained—Honey filtered through fine mesh to remove large foreign particles (such as wax) without removing the pollen. Strained honey is sometimes cloudy and will tend to form sugar crystals more easily than unstrained honey.

Whipped—Honey which has been processed to prevent crystallization. The presence of small crystals in the processed honey prevents the formation of larger crystals. Also called Spun Honey, Creamed Honey, and Honey Fondant.

STORING AND USING HONEY

Be sure to store honey in a dry cupboard, not in the refrigerator. Honey has a natural tendency to become grainy from the formation of sugar crystals. Cold can hasten the granulation process. If your honey becomes granulated, simply heat it in a pan of warm water to restore its freshness. When measuring honey for recipes, it can be helpful to grease your measuring spoons and cups with cooking spray or vegetable oil before measuring out the honey. This will prevent the honey from sticking to your utensils.

NUTRITIONAL INFORMATION

Everyone knows that honey is sweet, and indeed, honey is mostly made up of simple sugars (fructose and glucose). In fact, because honey is high in fructose, it has even stronger sweetening power than sugar. As a result, you can substitute less honey than sugar called for in a recipe and achieve the same sweetness.

There's a lot more to honey than its sweetness, however. Mother Nature's sweet treat contains no fat, no cholesterol, and no sodium. But it does contain vitamins, minerals, and antioxidants, including a particular antioxidant which is unique to honey, called pinocembrin. Furthermore, the glucose and fructose in honey make it particularly good as a source of energy. Unlike regular sugar, which gives a quick boost of energy and then causes a "sugar low," the combination of glucose and fructose in honey provides a more steady flow of energy. The glucose in honey is absorbed quickly and provides a fast energy boost. Thereafter, the fructose is absorbed more slowly and provides a lasting energy kick.

In addition to its nutritional value, honey has many other useful properties. Its antibiotic and antiseptic properties help burn victims to heal faster and with less scarring than with conventional burn treatments. It has antibacterial, antifungal, and anti-inflammatory elements, all useful in preventing infection, reducing pain, and improving circulation. Honey's viscosity is useful in a way you're probably very familiar with already: how many times have you soothed a sore throat by coating it with a spoonful of honey? Because honey absorbs moisture, it is also used as an ingredient in many cosmetic products, such as shampoos, moisturizing creams, skin cleansers, and conditioners.

WARNING: It is important to remember that children under one year old should not be given honey in any form (even cooked in recipes), because it contains elements which can lead to illness in infants. (Adults and older children have more developed digestive systems, which protect them against such illness.)

BREAKFAST

WHOLE WHEAT PANCAKES WITH CINNAMON HONEY BUTTER

Whole wheat flour is much higher in fiber than all-purpose flour, which means this breakfast is not only delicious, but good for you, too.

INGREDIENTS

Makes approximately 8 pancakes

Cinnamon Honey Butter:

1 tablespoon honey

3 tablespoons butter, softened

½ teaspoon cinnamon

Pancakes:

1 egg

¼ cup milk

1 tablespoon honey

½ cup whole wheat flour

2 tablespoons honey

PREPARATION

1. Prepare the butter: In a small bowl, combine the honey, butter, and cinnamon. Mix until smooth and blended. Refrigerate for at least 20 minutes.

2. Prepare the pancakes: In a medium bowl, whisk together the egg, milk, and honey until smooth.

3. Add the flour and mix until smooth.

4. Heat a large, heavy nonstick skillet over medium heat for 10 minutes, then reduce heat to low.

5. Use a ladle to pour 4-inch round pancakes onto the heated skillet, 1 inch apart.

6. Fry the pancakes until golden on each side.

7. Arrange the pancakes on a serving plate. Top each one with a generous dollop of Cinnamon Honey Butter and drizzle all with the 2 tablespoons of honey. Serve immediately.

FRUIT AND HONEY FRENCH TOAST

One of my favorite Sunday breakfast treats when I was growing up.

INGREDIENTS

Serves 2

French Toast:

½ cup milk

1 egg

½ tablespoon honey

½ teaspoon cinnamon

3 tablespoons butter

2 slices white bread, cut in half diagonally

Fruit and Honey Topping:

½ cup fresh strawberries

½ cup fresh orange slices

¼ cup crème fraîche

2 tablespoons honey

PREPARATION

1. In a medium bowl, combine the milk, egg, honey, cinnamon, and 2 tablespoons of butter. Mix with a fork until blended.

2. Heat a large nonstick skillet over medium heat.

3. Dunk 2 triangles of bread in the egg mixture and soak well.

4. Melt the remaining butter in the heated skillet, and fry the soaked bread until it is golden on each side.

5. Repeat steps 3 and 4 for the two remaining pieces of bread.

6. Arrange the French toast on two separate plates and garnish with the fresh fruit. Spoon half the crème fraîche on top of each plate. Garnish with honey and serve immediately.

HONEYED FRUIT BREAKFAST

When we eat this at our house, we love to pour yogurt over the fruit before sprinkling the granola on top. You may of course use any seasonal fruit you like.

INGREDIENTS

Serves 4

1 cup fresh strawberries, cut into ½-inch cubes

1 cup fresh orange slices

1 fresh apple, cut into ½-inch cubes

1 fresh pear, cut into ½-inch cubes

½ cup fresh cherries, pitted

1 tablespoon fresh mint leaves

3 tablespoons honey

1 cup granola or honey-flavored muesli

PREPARATION

1. In a large bowl, gently mix together the fruit, mint leaves, and honey. Set aside for 30 minutes to allow flavors to blend.

2. Spoon fruit into individual serving bowls and sprinkle granola or muesli on top. Serve immediately.

HONEY CHEESE-FILLED CRÊPES

Crêpes can be made in advance and refrigerated for up to 2 days. Fill them just before serving.

INGREDIENTS

Serves 2

Crêpes:

1 egg

¼ cup milk

1 tablespoon honey

⅓ cup flour

Filling:

1 cup cream cheese

3 tablespoons honey

½ cup raisins

2 tablespoons honey

PREPARATION

1. Heat a large, heavy nonstick skillet over medium heat for 10 minutes, then reduce heat to low.

2. Prepare the crêpes: In a small bowl, whisk together the egg, milk, and honey until smooth.

3. Add the flour and whisk until blended.

4. Spoon 2 tablespoons of crêpe batter into the heated skillet. Using a round spiral motion, pour the batter in a thin layer over the whole surface of the skillet.

5. Fry crêpe until golden, turning once. Transfer to a plate and set aside.

6. Repeat steps 4 and 5 until all the batter is gone.

7. Prepare the filling: Combine all the ingredients for the filling in a small bowl and mix well.

8. Place a crêpe on a clean work surface and spread on a generous layer of filling. Fold crêpe in half once, then again to form a small triangle with rounded top (see picture). Repeat to fill and fold all crêpes, transferring finished crêpes to individual serving plates. Place 2 crêpes on each plate.

9. Spoon a tablespoon of honey on each plate to garnish and serve immediately.

HONEY PANCAKES

Using honey instead of maple syrup makes an ordinary breakfast extraordinary.

INGREDIENTS

Makes approximately 8 pancakes

1 egg

¼ cup milk

1 tablespoon honey

½ cup flour

2 tablespoons honey

Confectioner's sugar
(for garnish)

PREPARATION

1. Heat a large, heavy skillet over medium heat for 10 minutes, then reduce heat to low.

2. In a medium bowl, whisk together egg, milk, and 1 tablespoon of honey until smooth.

3. Add the flour and mix until smooth.

4. Use a ladle to pour 4-inch round pancakes onto the heated skillet, 1 inch apart.

5. Fry the pancakes until they are golden on each side.

6. Arrange the pancakes on a serving plate and spoon the 2 tablespoons of honey in a spiral on top. Garnish with confectioner's sugar and serve.

HONEY CRUMPETS

To truly appreciate a crumpet, one must enjoy it with a cup of proper English tea—with milk, of course.

INGREDIENTS

Makes approximately 4 crumpets

1 egg

¼ cup milk

2 teaspoons fresh yeast

1 tablespoon honey

½ cup flour

2 tablespoons honey

PREPARATION

1. In a medium bowl, whisk together the egg, milk, yeast, and honey until smooth.

2. Add the flour, mix well, and set aside in a warm place to rise for 1 hour, or until bubbly.

3. Heat a large nonstick skillet over medium heat until hot, then reduce heat to low.

4. Use a ladle to spoon 4-inch round crumpets onto the heated skillet, 1 inch apart. Cover the skillet and let cook for 6 minutes. The crumpets will look like honeycomb when ready.

5. Arrange the crumpets on a serving plate and drizzle with honey. Serve immediately.

OATMEAL WITH APPLES AND HONEY

Another plain dish made superb with a touch of honey and some scrumptious fruit.

INGREDIENTS

Serves 4

1 apple, sliced very thin

1 cup milk

1 teaspoon cinnamon

¼ cup butter, softened

⅓ cup honey

1 cup whole oats

4 teaspoons honey

PREPARATION

1. Preheat oven to 400°F. Line a baking sheet with baking paper.

2. Arrange the apple slices on the prepared baking sheet. Bake for 15 minutes, or until golden brown.

3. In a small saucepan over medium heat, bring the milk and cinnamon to a boil.

4. Reduce heat and add the butter, honey, and oats. Cook, stirring constantly, until thick. Remove from heat and divide among individual serving bowls.

5. Arrange the baked apple slices atop each bowl, and spoon 1 teaspoon of honey on top.

6. Serve immediately.

SWEET POTATO PATTIES WITH HONEY CHEESE FILLING

These patties will be a big hit at your next Hannukah party. The delicious sweet potatoes add a splash of color to traditional Jewish latkes.

INGREDIENTS

Makes approximately 4 patties

Sweet Potato Patties:

1 pound sweet potatoes, peeled and finely grated

2 eggs

3 tablespoons cornstarch or potato flour

1 teaspoon salt

1 teaspoon white pepper

Honey Cheese Filling:

1 cup cream cheese

⅓ cup honey

1 teaspoon black pepper

½ teaspoon salt

2 cups vegetable oil for frying

1 tablespoon fresh dill

PREPARATION

1. Prepare the patties: Combine all the ingredients in a bowl and mix well. Refrigerate for a few minutes, until chilled.

2. Prepare the filling: Combine all the ingredients in a small bowl and mix well.

3. Preheat 2 cups of oil in a large skillet over medium heat.

4. Place spoonfuls of the sweet potato mixture into the oil ½ inch apart, gently flattening each ball with a metal spatula.

5. Fry patties until brown. Transfer to a paper towel to drain.

6. Arrange half of the fried patties on a serving plate. Place a teaspoon of filling in the center of each patty, garnish with dill, and place another patty on top. Serve immediately.

HONEY BAO
(CHINESE STEAMED BUNS)

Also called baozi. *These buns can be filled with meat or vegetables as well as fruit.*

INGREDIENTS

Makes 10 buns

Dough:

½ cup water

1 tablespoon fresh yeast

3 tablespoons honey

2 cups flour

1 teaspoon salt

2 tablespoons butter, softened

Filling:

½ cup honey

2 tablespoons pistachio paste (purchase online or in a gourmet store)

2 tablespoons pistachios, finely chopped

Extra flour

PREPARATION

1. Prepare the dough: In the bowl of a standing electric mixer with a dough hook attached, mix the water, yeast, honey, and flour on low speed for 3 minutes. Add the salt and butter, increase speed to medium, and mix for 5 minutes.

2. Transfer the dough to a floured bowl and refrigerate for 1 hour.

3. Prepare the filling: In a small bowl, mix all the ingredients together.

4. Assemble the buns: Divide the chilled dough into 10 equal portions; roll each portion into a ball; flatten each ball into a 4–5-inch round on a floured work surface. Place a tablespoon of filling in the center of each round and draw up sides around filling, pressing together to close.

5. Carefully arrange the buns in a single layer in a steamer basket lined with baking paper and let rise in a warm place for 1 hour, or until doubled in size. (If your steamer basket is not large enough to hold 10 buns at once, you may steam 2 batches separately.)

6. Fill a large pot at least halfway with water. Bring the water to a boil, place the steamer basket on top, and steam the buns for 20 minutes. Let cool for 15 minutes in the basket. Serve while still warm.

CINNAMON HONEY DONUTS

Make these donuts on a Saturday afternoon and save yourself a trip to the donut shop.

INGREDIENTS

Makes approximately 10 donuts

1 tablespoon fresh yeast

¼ cup water

¼ cup cold milk

3 tablespoons honey

2 cups flour

1 teaspoon cinnamon

1 teaspoon salt

¼ cup butter, softened

6 cups vegetable oil for frying

2 tablespoons honey

Extra flour

PREPARATION

1. In the bowl of a standing electric mixer with a dough hook attached, mix the yeast, water, milk, honey, and flour on low speed for 3 minutes. Add the cinnamon, salt, and butter, increase the speed to medium, and mix for 5 minutes.

2. Transfer the dough to a floured bowl, cover with a clean kitchen towel, and let rise in a warm spot for 1 hour, or until doubled in size.

3. Punch down the risen dough and transfer to a floured work surface. Roll out to ½ inch thick. Use a cup or cookie cutter to cut 3-inch rounds from the dough. Gather the excess, roll into a ball, and roll out again. Continue cutting and re-rolling the excess until all the dough is used. Transfer the rounds to a lightly floured cutting board or place mat and let rise for 2 hours at room temperature, or until doubled in size.

4. In a large, deep pan or skillet, heat the oil to 360°F. Fry the dough rounds until golden brown. Transfer to a paper towel to drain.

5. Arrange the fried donuts on a serving plate and drizzle with honey to garnish. Serve while still warm.

32

HONEY AND BLUE-CHEESE BRUSCHETTA

The word bruschetta *derives from the Roman word* bruscare, *which means "to roast over coals."*

Serves 4

½ loaf French bread or baguette (approximately 12 inches long)

3 ounces blue cheese

2 tablespoons honey

1 tablespoon walnuts, crushed

1. Preheat the oven to 400°F.

2. Slice the bread into ¼-inch slices.

3. Arrange the bread slices on a dry baking sheet and toast for 4–5 minutes or until the bread is golden brown. Turn the slices and toast for another 4–5 minutes until browned.

4. Remove the toasted bread slices from the oven and let cool for 5 minutes.

5. Crumble the blue cheese over the toasted bread slices, spoon a generous amount of honey on top, and garnish with the crushed walnuts.

6. Arrange on a serving platter and serve.

BAKED GOODS

HONEY CAKE WITH CARAMELIZED ORANGES

If you've never tried them, the flavor of caramelized oranges will definitely surprise and delight you.

INGREDIENTS

Serves 6

1½ cups honey

2 small oranges, sliced into ½-inch slices

1½ cups butter

½ teaspoon salt

3 eggs

½ cup freshly squeezed orange juice

2 teaspoons orange zest

½ cup flour

¾ cup blanched almonds, ground

1 teaspoon baking powder

Extra butter

PREPARATION

1. Heat a medium skillet over medium heat. Add ½ cup of honey and orange slices, reduce heat to low, and cook for 30 minutes, or until the oranges turn golden brown. Remove the pan from heat and set aside.

2. In a large bowl, beat together the butter, salt, remaining honey, and eggs with an electric mixer on medium speed, until the mixture is smooth and light. Add the orange juice and zest and mix until thoroughly blended.

3. Fold in the flour, almonds, and baking powder with a spatula. Cover the bowl with plastic wrap and refrigerate for at least 2 hours.

4. Preheat oven to 375°F. Grease an 8-inch round baking pan.

5. Arrange the caramelized orange slices in the bottom of the prepared pan. Pour in the batter. Bake for 45 minutes, or until golden brown.

6. Let the cake cool in the pan for 15 minutes, then flip over onto a serving plate and gently jiggle pan to remove. Let cool completely before serving. Store for up to 2 days in an airtight container at room temperature.

ICED HONEY MUFFINS

Instead of the icing, you can top these muffins with fresh butter or jelly.

INGREDIENTS

Makes 12 muffins

Muffins:

1 cup butter, softened

¾ cup honey

2 eggs

½ cup sweet cream

1½ cups flour

½ teaspoon ground nutmeg

2 teaspoons baking powder

Icing:

2 egg whites

1 cup confectioner's sugar

PREPARATION

1. Preheat oven to 375°F. Grease 12 muffin cups with 1 tablespoon of butter, or fit holes with disposable muffin cups.

2. Prepare the muffins: In a large bowl, cream together butter and honey with an electric mixer on medium speed.

3. Add the remaining ingredients. Reduce the mixer speed to low and mix until blended.

4. Divide batter evenly among the 12 cups of the muffin tin. Bake for 20 minutes.

5. Prepare the icing: With an electric mixer, beat the egg whites and sugar together until thick.

6. Remove the muffins from oven and set aside to cool completely in the pan.

7. Spoon a generous amount of icing on each muffin. Store for up to 24 hours at room temperature in an airtight container.

HONEY LIME TARTS

Use freshly squeezed lime juice for maximum flavor.

INGREDIENTS

Makes 4 individual tarts

Crust:

½ cup butter, chilled

2 tablespoons confectioner's sugar

1 egg

1 tablespoon cold water

½ teaspoon salt

1½ cups flour

Filling:

1 cup lime juice

¾ cup honey

5 egg yolks

Extra flour

Extra butter

1 egg, beaten

PREPARATION

1. Prepare the crust: In a large bowl, cream together the butter and sugar with an electric mixer on high, for about 2 minutes, or until smooth. Stop the mixer occasionally to scrape the sides of the bowl with a spatula.

2. Add the egg, water, and salt and mix for 2 minutes, or until blended. Add the flour and mix for 1 minute, or until the mixture forms a ball of dough.

3. Remove the dough from the bowl and wrap tightly with plastic wrap. Refrigerate for at least 1 hour before using.

4. Transfer the chilled dough to a floured work surface. Roll out to an 11 x 11-inch square, ⅛ inch thick. Cut into 4 equal squares.

5. Transfer each square to a greased 4-inch individual tart pan and gently press into shape with your fingers. Trim off the edges of the dough. (You may roll trimmings into a ball, wrap with plastic wrap, and store in the freezer for up to 1 month.) Refrigerate for 15 minutes. Preheat oven to 375°F.

6. Cut 4 circles of baking paper to cover the bottom of each tart crust and place 1 in each pan. Place baking weights/beans on top. Bake for 15 minutes.

7. Remove the baking weights/beans and paper circles. Brush the crusts with the beaten egg. Bake for 3 minutes more, then remove from the oven, and set aside to cool completely. Turn oven temperature down to 350°F.

8. Prepare the filling: In a medium bowl, whisk together all the ingredients.

9. Pour into the baked tart shells.

10. Bake for 20 minutes. Let cool completely before serving. Store in the refrigerator for up to 2 days. Serve at room temperature.

HONEY SCONES

Serve these delicious scones topped with jam or marmalade.

INGREDIENTS

Makes 12 scones

⅓ cup butter, softened

3 tablespoons sugar

¼ cup cold milk

1 egg + 1 egg yolk

2½ cups flour

2 teaspoons baking powder

½ cup honey

pinch salt

extra flour

PREPARATION

1. In a large bowl, blend the butter and sugar with an electric mixer on low speed, until smooth.

2. Add the milk, egg, and egg yolk and continue to mix. Add the flour, baking powder, honey, and salt and mix until you have a smooth dough.

3. Transfer the dough to a lightly floured work surface and divide into 12 equal portions.

4. Lightly flour your hands and roll each portion of dough into a ball, then gently flatten to form ½-inch-wide ovals.

5. Arrange the ovals ½ inch apart on a baking sheet lined with baking paper. Set aside to rest for 30 minutes.

6. Preheat oven to 375°F.

7. Bake for 15 minutes, or until scones are golden brown. Set aside to cool for 20 minutes.

8. Store for up to 24 hours in an airtight container at room temperature. Warm before serving.

HONEY AND FRUIT-FILLED BRIOCHES

Brioche *comes from the Old French word* broyer *or* brier, *which means* "to knead."

INGREDIENTS

Makes 12 brioches

Dough:

1 tablespoon fresh yeast

¼ cup water

1 egg

3 tablespoons sugar

2 cups flour

1 teaspoon salt

⅓ cup butter, softened

Filling:

¾ cup honey

½ cup dried apricots, cut into small cubes

½ cup prunes, cut into small cubes

⅓ cup raisins

¼ cup pistachios

Extra flour

PREPARATION

1. Prepare the dough: In the bowl of a standing electric mixer fitted with a dough hook, combine the yeast, water, egg, sugar, and flour. Mix for 3 minutes on low speed.

2. Add the salt and butter and mix for 5 minutes on medium speed.

3. Transfer the dough to a floured bowl and refrigerate for 1 hour.

4. Assemble the brioche: On a lightly floured work surface, roll out the dough to a thin rectangle, about 13 by 8 inches.

5. Use a rubber spatula to spread honey evenly over the surface of the dough. Sprinkle the fruit and pistachios over the top to cover the whole surface.

6. Starting from one long side of the rectangle, roll the dough up halfway. Then roll up from the opposite side, forming two spirals side by side.

7. Use a sharp knife to slice the dough into 12 equal pieces. Place each piece in a greased or lined muffin cup, filling side up. Set aside in a warm place to rise for 1 hour.

8. Preheat oven to 375°F.

9. Bake for 15 minutes, or until golden brown. Let cool for 10 minutes before serving, or store for up to 1 day in an airtight container at room temperature. Reheat before serving.

SPICED HONEY BREAD

Try making a peanut butter and jelly sandwich with this delicious loaf and you'll never go back to white bread again.

INGREDIENTS

Serves 6

1 cup cold milk

1 tablespoon dry yeast

1 large egg

½ cup honey

¼ cup butter

2½ cups flour

2 teaspoons salt

½ teaspoon cinnamon

½ teaspoon ground cloves

1 egg, beaten (for brushing)

⅓ cup sesame seeds

Extra flour

PREPARATION

1. In the bowl of a standing electric mixer with a dough hook attached, mix the milk, yeast, egg, honey, butter, and flour on low speed for 3 minutes. Add the salt, cinnamon, and cloves, increase speed to medium, and mix for 6 minutes. (At this stage, you may wrap the dough in plastic wrap and store in the freezer for up to 1 week. Defrost at room temperature and continue from step 2.)

2. Transfer the dough to a floured bowl, cover with plastic wrap, and let rise at room temperature for 1 hour, or until the dough has doubled in size.

3. Punch down the risen dough and transfer to a floured work surface. Lightly flour your hands, then flatten the dough with your palms. Divide into 3 equal portions and roll each portion into a ball. Let the dough rest for 5 minutes.

4. Roll each ball into a 15-inch-long cylinder. Braid cylinders together to form a loaf, tucking ends underneath to seal.

5. Transfer the braided loaf to a baking sheet lined with baking paper. Brush with the beaten egg and sprinkle sesame seeds on top. Let rise for 1½ hours.

6. Preheat oven to 375°F. Bake the loaf for 30 minutes, or until golden brown. Transfer the loaf to a metal rack and let cool for at least 30 minutes before slicing. Store for up to 2 days in a bread box.

WHOLE WHEAT HONEY BREAD

For a delicious afternoon snack, toast this lightly sweet bread and serve with orange preserves and a cup of tea.

INGREDIENTS

Serves 6

1½ cups cold water

2 teaspoons dry yeast

⅓ cup honey

3 cups whole wheat flour

1 tablespoon salt

¼ cup butter, softened

Extra flour

Extra butter

PREPARATION

1. In the bowl of a standing electric mixer with a dough hook attached, mix together the water, yeast, honey, and flour on low speed for 3 minutes.

2. Add the salt and butter, increase speed to medium, and mix for 6 minutes.

3. Transfer the dough to a floured bowl, cover with a clean kitchen towel, and set aside to rise at room temperature for 1 hour, or until the dough has doubled in size.

4. Punch down the risen dough and transfer to a floured work surface. Lightly flour your hands, then shape the dough into a ball. Roll the ball into a cylindrical loaf and transfer to a greased loaf pan. Let rise in a warm spot for 1 hour, or until the dough has doubled in size.

5. Preheat oven to 425°F. Bake the loaf for 40 minutes, or until a tap on the loaf produces a hollow sound. Serve hot, or store in a bread box for up to 2 days.

GOAT CHEESE–STUFFED HONEY RYE LOAF

You may substitute fromage blanc or bucheron for goat cheese, but definitely use fresh cheese whenever possible.

INGREDIENTS

Serves 6

1½ cups cold water

2 teaspoons dry yeast

¼ cup honey

2½ cups bread flour

1 cup rye flour

1 tablespoon salt

½ cup dried cranberries

One 9-ounce wheel fresh goat cheese, halved

Extra flour

PREPARATION

1. In the bowl of a standing electric mixer with a dough hook attached, mix together the water, yeast, honey, and flours on low speed for 3 minutes.

2. Add the salt and cranberries, increase speed to medium, and mix for 6 minutes.

3. Transfer the dough to a floured bowl, cover with a clean kitchen towel, and set aside to rise at room temperature for 1 hour, or until the dough has doubled in size.

4. Punch down the risen dough and transfer to a floured work surface. Roll out to ¾ inch thick.

5. Place the cheese halves end-to-end in the center of the dough and roll up like a roulade. Transfer to a baking sheet lined with baking paper and let rise in a warm spot for 1 hour, or until the dough has doubled in size.

6. Preheat oven to 350°F. Bake the loaf for 35–40 minutes, or until a tap on the loaf produces a hollow sound. Let cool completely before slicing. Store the baked bread for up to 2 days in a bread box.

ORANGE HONEY ALMOND CAKE

To give this cake the best flavor possible, I recommend using Cointreau or Grand Marnier for the orange liqueur.

INGREDIENTS

Serves 6

¾ cup candied citrus peels

1 tablespoon orange liqueur

1 cup butter

½ teaspoon salt

1 cup honey

3 eggs

½ cup freshly squeezed orange juice

2 teaspoons orange zest

¾ cup flour

½ cup blanched almonds, ground

1 teaspoon baking powder

Syrup:

2 tablespoons sugar dissolved in 2 tablespoons boiling water

Extra butter

PREPARATION

1. Prepare the cake: In a small bowl, combine the citrus peels and liqueur. Let soak for 1 hour at room temperature.

2. In a large bowl, beat together the butter, salt, honey, and eggs with an electric mixer on medium, until the mixture is smooth and light. Add the orange juice and zest and blend well.

3. Fold in the flour, almonds, and baking powder with a spatula. Remove at least 15 citrus peels from the soaking bowl and set aside for garnish. Drain the remaining peels and fold them into the cake batter. Cover the batter bowl with plastic wrap and refrigerate for at least 2 hours.

4. Preheat oven to 375°F. Grease a 9-inch Bundt pan.

5. Scatter 15 reserved orange peels around the bottom of the prepared pan. Pour in the chilled batter, filling the pan no more than ¾ full. Bake for 45 minutes, or until the cake is golden brown.

6. Let the cake cool in the pan for 15 minutes, then remove from the pan, and transfer to a metal rack to cool completely. Transfer the cooled cake to a serving platter, and drizzle with syrup. Let stand for at least 10 minutes before slicing. Store in an airtight container at room temperature for up to 2 days.

HONEY PUMPKIN COOKIES

*To make these for your next Halloween party, use pumpkin-shaped cookie cutters
and decorate with colored icing.*

INGREDIENTS

Makes approximately 40 cookies

¾ cup butter

½ cup honey

2 eggs

1 teaspoon vanilla extract

2 tablespoons brandy

1 teaspoon salt

1½ cups flour

1 teaspoon baking powder

½ cup fresh pumpkin, finely grated

¼ cup toasted pumpkin seeds, chopped

Extra flour

1 egg, beaten

PREPARATION

1. In the bowl of a food processor fitted with a metal blade, blend together the butter and honey for 2 minutes, or until smooth. Add the eggs, vanilla, brandy, salt, half the flour, and all of the baking powder, and process for 2 minutes. Add the remaining flour and process for 1 minute. Add the pumpkin and pumpkin seeds and process until the mixture forms a ball of dough.

2. Wrap the dough in plastic wrap and refrigerate for at least 30 minutes.

3. Preheat oven to 375°F. Line a baking sheet with baking paper.

4. Transfer the chilled dough to a floured work surface and roll out to ⅛ inch thick. Use a sharp knife to cut 1 x ½-inch rectangles. Gather the trimmings, roll into a ball, and roll out again to cut more rectangles. Continue to cut and re-roll until all the dough is used.

5. Arrange the rectangles ½ inch apart on the prepared baking sheet and brush the tops with the beaten egg. Bake for 15 minutes. Transfer the cookies to a metal rack to cool completely before serving. Store for up to 1 week in an airtight container.

BAKED HONEY CHEESECAKE

Beautiful and tasty, this cake is a crowd-pleaser.

INGREDIENTS

Makes one 10-inch round cake

Crust:

1 cup butter, softened

1 cup graham crackers, finely crushed

½ cup packed brown sugar

Filling:

6 eggs, separated

1 pound light cream cheese

1½ cups honey

3 tablespoons cornstarch

2 tablespoons pistachios, chopped

PREPARATION

1. Preheat oven to 325°F.

2. Prepare the crust: In a medium bowl, blend together all the ingredients. Set aside.

3. Prepare the filling: In a large bowl, beat the egg yolks with an electric mixer on high, until thick. Add the cheese and mix until blended. Mix in the honey and cornstarch.

4. In a separate bowl, beat the egg whites with an electric mixer on high, until they form stiff peaks.

5. Gently fold the beaten egg whites into the rest of the filling mixture with a spatula.

6. Spread the graham cracker crust evenly onto the bottom of a 10-inch round baking pan, pressing down firmly with your fingers. Pour in the filling and level the top with a spatula or palette knife. Bake for 1 hour.

7. Cool the baked cake at room temperature for 1 hour, then refrigerate for 2 hours. Store in an airtight container in the refrigerator for up to 3 days. Sprinkle with pistachios before serving.

HONEY APPLE TARTS

*Apples and honey are a common flavor combination, but they'll hardly seem
common in this scrumptious dessert.*

INGREDIENTS

Makes 4 individual tarts

Crust:

½ cup butter, chilled

2 tablespoons confectioner's
sugar

1 egg

1 tablespoon cold water

½ teaspoon salt

1½ cups flour

Extra flour

Extra butter

1 egg, beaten

Filling:

¾ cup honey

6 medium apples, peeled and
sliced very thin

1 cup sweet cream

4 egg yolks

PREPARATION

1. Prepare the crust: In a large
bowl, cream together the butter
and sugar with an electric mixer
on high, for about 2 minutes,
or until smooth. Stop the mixer
occasionally to scrape the sides
of the bowl with a spatula.

2. Add the egg, water, and salt
and mix for 2 minutes, or until
blended. Add the flour and mix
for 1 minute, or until the
mixture forms a ball of dough.

3. Remove the dough from the
bowl and wrap tightly with
plastic wrap. Refrigerate for at
least 1 hour before using.

4. Transfer the chilled dough
to a floured work surface.
Roll out to an 11 x 11-inch
square, ⅛ inch thick. Cut
into 4 equal squares.

5. Transfer each square to a
greased 4-inch individual tart pan
and gently press into shape with
your fingers. Trim off the edges
of the dough. (You may roll the
trimmings into a ball, wrap with
plastic wrap, and store in the
freezer for up to 1 month.)
Refrigerate for 15 minutes.
Preheat oven to 375°F.

6. Cut 4 circles of baking paper
to cover the bottom of each tart
crust and place one in each pan.
Place baking weights/beans on
top. Bake for 15 minutes.

7. Remove the baking
weights/beans and paper circles.
Brush the crusts with the beaten
egg. Bake for 3 minutes more,
then remove from the oven, and
set aside to cool completely.
(Turn off the oven.)

(continued on page 56)

(continued from page 54)

HONEY CARROT CAKE WITH PEARS

The pears make this carrot cake extra moist.

8. Prepare the filling: Heat a large skillet over medium heat. Add the honey and bring to a boil.

9. Add the apples and cook for 20 minutes, or until golden brown, stirring occasionally.

10. Preheat oven to 350°F. Using a slotted spoon, transfer the apples from the skillet to the baked tart shells. Transfer the liquid left in the skillet to a medium bowl.

11. Add to the cooking liquid the cream and egg yolks, and whisk together until blended.

12. Pour the cream-egg mixture into tart shells, filling each one until just below top of crust. Take care not to overfill. Bake for 20 minutes. Let cool completely before serving. Store in the refrigerator for up to 2 days. Serve at room temperature.

INGREDIENTS

Serves 6

1 cup butter, softened

1 cup honey

½ cup packed brown sugar

2 eggs

1 cup flour

2 teaspoons baking powder

1 teaspoon cinnamon

1 cup carrots, finely grated

3 ripe pears, cut into ½-inch cubes

Extra butter

PREPARATION

1. Preheat oven to 375°F. Grease a 12-inch loaf pan.

2. In a large bowl, combine the butter, honey, and brown sugar with an electric mixer on medium speed, for 2 minutes, or until blended. Add the eggs, flour, baking powder, and cinnamon, reduce the speed to low, and mix until blended.

3. Fold in the carrots and pears with a spatula.

4. Pour the batter into the prepared pan. Bake for 35–40 minutes, or until a toothpick inserted in the center of the cake comes out clean. Let cool completely before serving. Store for up to 2 days in an airtight container at room temperature.

HONEY PRUNE COOKIES

My grandmother gave me the recipe for these cookies and told me that her grandmother had given it to her when she was just a girl.

INGREDIENTS

Makes approximately 40 cookies

¾ cup butter

½ cup honey

2 eggs

1 teaspoon vanilla extract

2 tablespoons brandy

1 teaspoon salt

1½ cups flour

1 teaspoon baking powder

¼ cup finely chopped prunes

Extra flour

1 egg, beaten

PREPARATION

1. In a food processor fitted with a metal blade, blend together the butter and honey for 2 minutes, or until smooth. Add the eggs, vanilla, brandy, salt, half the flour, and all of the baking powder, and process for 2 minutes. Add the remaining flour and process for 1 minute. Add the prunes and process until the mixture forms a ball of dough.

2. Wrap the dough in plastic wrap and refrigerate for at least 30 minutes.

3. Preheat oven to 375°F. Line a baking sheet with baking paper.

4. Transfer the chilled dough to a floured work surface and roll out to ⅛ inch thick. Use a sharp knife to cut 1-inch squares. Gather trimmings, roll into a ball, and roll out again to cut more squares. Continue to cut and re-roll until all the dough is used.

5. Arrange the squares ½ inch apart on a prepared baking sheet and brush the tops with the beaten egg. Bake for 15 minutes. Transfer the cookies to a metal rack to cool completely before serving. Store for up to 1 week in an airtight container at room temperature.

TRADITIONAL JEWISH HONEY CAKE

It is customary to eat honey on the Jewish New Year (called in Hebrew Rosh Hashanah) *to ensure a sweet year.*

INGREDIENTS

Makes one 12 x 4-inch loaf

1 cup butter, softened

½ cup brown sugar

3 eggs

1 cup honey

1½ cups flour

2 teaspoons baking powder

1 tablespoon instant coffee dissolved in 1 tablespoon boiling water

1 teaspoon cinnamon

¾ cup whole walnuts

½ cup dried cranberries

Extra butter

PREPARATION

1. Preheat oven to 375°F. Grease a 12 x 4-inch loaf pan.

2. In a large bowl, cream together the butter and brown sugar with an electric mixer on medium speed, for about 2 minutes, or until smooth.

3. Add the eggs, honey, flour, baking powder, coffee, and cinnamon and reduce the mixer speed to low. Mix until blended.

4. Fold in the walnuts and cranberries with a spatula.

5. Pour the batter into the prepared pan. Bake for 35 minutes, or until a toothpick inserted in the center of the cake comes out clean. Let cool completely in the pan before slicing.

6. Store for up to 2 days in an airtight container at room temperature.

CRISPY HONEY ALMOND COOKIES

Enjoy these cookies with a cup of your favorite coffee for a great afternoon snack.

INGREDIENTS

Makes approximately 25 cookies

2 egg whites

1 cup honey

1½ cups blanched almonds, coarsely ground

3 tablespoons flour

¼ cup Amaretto

PREPARATION

1. Preheat oven to 375°F. Line a baking sheet with baking paper.

2. In a medium bowl, beat the egg whites with an electric mixer on high until they form soft peaks. Gradually add the honey and beat until the mixture stiffens.

3. Gradually fold in the ground almonds with a spatula. Gently fold in the flour and Amaretto and mix until blended.

4. Spoon 1-inch rounds onto the prepared baking sheet, 2 inches apart.

5. Bake for 15 minutes, or until golden brown. Transfer the cookies to a metal rack to cool completely. Store for up to 1 week in an airtight container at room temperature.

SALADS AND ENTRÉES

HONEY CITRUS SALAD

Refreshing and colorful, this salad is great for a summer brunch.

INGREDIENTS

Serves 4

1 red grapefruit, peeled and cut into ½-inch cubes

1 yellow grapefruit, peeled and cut into ½-inch cubes

2 oranges, peeled and cut into ½-inch cubes

2 clementines or mandarin oranges, peeled and cut into ½-inch cubes

3 tablespoons honey

1 tablespoon citrus liqueur or brandy

PREPARATION

1. Combine all the ingredients in a large bowl and mix well. Refrigerate for at least 1 hour and no more than 2 hours, to allow flavors to blend.

2. Remove from the refrigerator and transfer to individual serving bowls. Serve immediately.

HONEY WALDORF SALAD

This salad was extremely popular in the '70s and '80s. It's been updated here to please the modern palate.

INGREDIENTS

Serves 4

Dressing:

1 teaspoon salt

1 teaspoon ground black pepper

1 tablespoon mayonnaise

1 tablespoon sour cream

1 teaspoon mustard

3 tablespoons honey

Salad:

2 stalks celery, cut into ½-inch cubes

2 apples, cut into ½-inch cubes

2 pears, cut into ½-inch cubes

2 bananas, cut into ½-inch cubes

½ cup toasted walnuts, broken into large pieces

PREPARATION

1. Prepare the dressing: Combine all the ingredients in a small jar with a lid, and shake until blended. Set aside.

2. Prepare the salad: Place all the ingredients in a large bowl, pour the dressing on top, and mix well.

3. Refrigerate for at least 1 hour, or store for up to 24 hours in the refrigerator. If the salad has been in the refrigerator longer than 1 hour, let it sit at room temperature for 20 minutes before serving.

4. Spoon the salad into individual serving bowls and serve immediately.

PERSONAL CAESAR SALAD WITH HONEY DRESSING

Chef Caesar Cardini is credited with creating Caesar salad when a Fourth of July rush of customers at his Tijuana restaurant forced him to use whatever ingredients he had on hand.

INGREDIENTS

Serves 2

Salad:

1 pound hearts of romaine lettuce

1 tablespoon capers, finely chopped

2 ripe tomatoes, cut into 8 pieces (optional)

Dressing:

1 tablespoon smooth Dijon mustard

3 tablespoons honey

1 tablespoon balsamic vinegar

¼ cup olive oil

1 tablespoon anchovy fillets, finely chopped

1 teaspoon salt

1 teaspoon ground white pepper

½ pound cooked chicken breast, cut into strips

2 tablespoons Parmesan cheese, grated

PREPARATION

1. Prepare the salad: Place the lettuce, capers, and tomatoes in a large serving bowl.

2. Prepare the dressing: In a small bowl, whisk together the mustard, honey, and vinegar until smooth.

3. Whisking constantly, gradually add the olive oil.

4. Add the anchovies, salt, and pepper. Mix well.

5. Pour dressing on salad and toss lightly to coat.

6. Transfer salad to 2 small salad plates. Arrange the chicken on top of the salads and sprinkle with the Parmesan. Serve immediately.

CARROT SALAD WITH LIGHT HONEY DRESSING

You may roughly grate the carrots instead of cutting them for this salad.

INGREDIENTS

Serves 4

Salad

2 pounds carrots, peeled and cut into thin strips

2 tablespoons parsley, chopped

2 tablespoons spring onion, finely chopped

Dressing

1 tablespoon smooth Dijon mustard

3 tablespoons honey

1 tablespoon red wine vinegar

¼ cup olive oil

1 teaspoon salt

1 teaspoon ground white pepper

3 tablespoons raw sunflower seeds, shelled

PREPARATION

1. Prepare the salad: Place the carrots, parsley, and spring onion in a large serving bowl.

2. Prepare the dressing: In a small bowl, whisk together the mustard, honey, and vinegar until smooth.

3. Whisking constantly, gradually add the olive oil.

4. Add salt and pepper. Mix well.

5. Pour the dressing over the salad and toss to coat. Sprinkle sunflower seeds on top and serve immediately.

GREEN SALAD WITH HONEY CITRUS VINAIGRETTE

Adding leftover roast chicken or even cubes of your favorite cheese will turn this light, refreshing salad into a filling meal.

INGREDIENTS

Serves 2

Salad

1 pound salad greens

½ cup cherry tomatoes, halved

Dressing

1 tablespoon strong Dijon mustard

3 tablespoons honey

1 tablespoon balsamic vinegar

3 tablespoons olive oil

3 tablespoons orange juice

1 teaspoon salt

1 teaspoon ground white pepper

PREPARATION

1. Prepare the salad: Place the salad greens and tomatoes in a large bowl.

2. Prepare the dressing: In a small bowl, whisk together the mustard, honey, and balsamic vinegar until smooth.

3. Whisking constantly, gradually add the olive oil, followed by orange juice.

4. Add the salt and pepper and whisk until blended.

5. Pour the dressing over the salad and lightly toss to coat. Serve immediately.

HONEY AND MUSTARD SEED PORK BREAST

Mustard seed has been used as a spice since 800 AD. Here it imparts a delicious flavor as well as a beautiful coating for the pork.

INGREDIENTS

Serves 12

2 tablespoons Dijon mustard, with seeds

3 tablespoons honey

2 tablespoons olive oil

1 tablespoon fresh thyme, chopped

2 teaspoons garlic, chopped

2 teaspoons ground black pepper

2 teaspoons salt

2 teaspoons mustard seeds

One 6-pound pork breast

PREPARATION

1. Preheat oven to 400°F. In a small bowl, combine all the ingredients except the mustard seeds and meat and mix together until smooth.

2. Place the pork in a roasting pan and coat with sauce on all sides. Sprinkle mustard seeds on top and sides and lightly press with your hands.

3. Wrap the pork in aluminum foil and cook for 15 minutes, then reduce heat to 375°F and continue to cook for another 1½ hours.

4. Remove the aluminum foil and cook for another 30 minutes.

5. Transfer the cooked pork to a cutting board and let rest for 10 minutes.

6. Use a sharp knife to slice the pork into slices ⅓ inch thick. Serve immediately.

HONEY-GLAZED CHICKEN BREASTS

For attractive presentation, serve this dish on a bed of lettuce or on top of your favorite salad.

INGREDIENTS

Serves 2

1 tablespoon smooth Dijon mustard

3 tablespoons honey

1 teaspoon soy sauce

2 tablespoons sunflower oil

1 teaspoon salt

1 teaspoon ground black pepper

Two 10–12-ounce chicken breasts

PREPARATION

1. Preheat oven to 425°F. Line a small baking dish with baking paper.

2. In a small bowl, combine all the ingredients except for the chicken and mix until smooth.

3. Arrange the chicken breasts in the prepared pan and pour over the glaze, making sure to coat the chicken on all sides. Bake for 15 minutes, or until the chicken's juices run clear.

4. Transfer breasts to a cutting board and slice into strips ⅓ inch thick. Serve immediately.

HONEY-COATED FISH WITH SOY SAUCE

This succulent fish is best served on a bed of steamed green vegetables.

INGREDIENTS

Serves 4

3 tablespoons honey

2 teaspoons soy sauce

½ teaspoon sesame oil

1 teaspoon fresh ginger, finely chopped

1 teaspoon ground white pepper

Four 8-ounce fillets of your favorite white fish

PREPARATION

1. Preheat oven to 425°F.

2. In a small bowl, combine all the ingredients except the fish and mix well.

3. Arrange fish in a roasting pan, pour over the sauce, and cook for 15 minutes, or until meat can be flaked with a fork. Serve immediately.

HONEY CHILI WINGS

Try making these for your next big game party and watch them disappear as fast as you can cook them.

INGREDIENTS

Serves 4

½ cup honey

1 tablespoon fresh red chili pepper, finely chopped

1 tablespoon garlic, chopped

1 teaspoon salt

2 tablespoons soy sauce

3 tablespoons butter, melted

30 chicken wings

PREPARATION

1. Preheat oven to 400°F.

2. In a large bowl, combine all the ingredients except the wings and mix well.

3. Add the wings and mix to coat.

4. Arrange on a baking sheet and cook for 20 minutes, or until juices run clear.

5. Transfer the cooked wings to a serving platter and serve immediately.

CRISPY CALAMARI WITH HONEY SAUCE

Thai chili sauce is available in most large grocery stores and Asian specialty shops.

INGREDIENTS

Serves 4

Sauce:

¼ cup honey

2 tablespoons sweet Thai chili sauce

1 tablespoon lemon juice

1 teaspoon salt

4 cups frying oil

Calamari:

½ cup breadcrumbs

1 cup flour

1 teaspoon Spanish paprika

1 teaspoon salt

1 teaspoon ground white pepper

2 pounds small calamari, cut into ⅓-inch rings

PREPARATION

1. Prepare the sauce: In a small bowl, combine all the ingredients and mix well.

2. Prepare the calamari: In a medium bowl, combine the breadcrumbs, flour, paprika, salt, and pepper and mix well.

3. Heat the oil in a deep skillet or pot over medium heat. Test the heat by dropping crumbs into the oil: when they fry immediately, the oil is ready.

4. Dredge half the calamari in the breadcrumb coating. Shake off the excess.

5. Fry until golden and crispy.

6. Transfer to a paper towel to drain.

7. Repeat steps 4 through 6 with the remaining calamari.

8. Transfer the fried calamari to a serving platter. Pour over the sauce and serve immediately.

STIR-FRIED PORK IN SPICED HONEY SAUCE

This dish is especially delicious served on a bed of steamed white rice.

INGREDIENTS

Serves 2

2 tablespoons sunflower oil

1 pound pork, cut into chunks

¼ cup onion, chopped

½ tablespoon garlic, chopped

1 tablespoon fresh ginger, grated

3 tablespoons honey

1 teaspoon soy sauce

1 teaspoon salt

1 teaspoon ground black pepper

2 tablespoons fresh coriander, finely chopped

PREPARATION

1. Heat a large skillet or wok over high heat.

2. Add the oil, pork, and onion, and cook until the pork browns, stirring constantly.

3. Add the garlic and ginger and cook for 2 minutes.

4. Add the honey, soy sauce, salt, and pepper and cook 5 minutes.

5. Remove from heat and stir in the coriander. Serve immediately, or store in the refrigerator for up to 24 hours. Reheat before serving.

LAMB WITH HONEY AND SPICES

Serve this superb entrée with steamed vegetables or baked potatoes.

INGREDIENTS

Serves 8

1 tablespoon smooth Dijon mustard

3 tablespoons honey

2 tablespoons olive oil

1 tablespoon fresh rosemary, chopped

2 teaspoons garlic, chopped

2 teaspoons ground black pepper

2 teaspoons salt

One 5-pound lamb thigh

PREPARATION

1. Preheat oven to 450°F

2. In a small bowl, combine all the ingredients except for the lamb and mix until smooth.

3. Place the lamb thigh in a roasting pan and coat with sauce on all sides. Bake for 15 minutes.

4. Reduce heat to 375°F and continue to cook for another 1–1½ hours, until a meat thermometer inserted in the center of the thigh reads 130–140°F.

5. Transfer the cooked thigh to a cutting board and let rest for 10 minutes.

6. Use a sharp knife to slice the meat into slices ⅓ inch thick. Serve immediately.

HONEY MEATBALLS

Regular meatballs are transformed into a gourmet treat with a delightful honey sauce.

INGREDIENTS

Serves 4

Meatballs:

1½ pounds lean ground veal

1 egg

⅓ cup breadcrumbs

1 teaspoon fine salt

½ teaspoon ground white pepper

Sauce:

2 tablespoons olive oil

1 medium onion, finely chopped

1 celery stalk, finely chopped

2 teaspoons garlic, chopped

½ cup honey

1 cup white wine

1 tablespoon Spanish paprika

2 teaspoons salt

1 teaspoon ground white pepper

PREPARATION

1. Prepare the meatballs: In a large bowl, combine all the ingredients and mix well.

2. Roll meat into 2-inch round balls and set aside.

3. Prepare the sauce: Heat a large pot over medium heat. Add the olive oil, onion, and celery and cook until golden.

4. Add the garlic and cook for 3 minutes.

5. Add the remaining sauce ingredients and bring to a boil.

6. Add meatballs and cover. Reduce heat to low and cook for 30 minutes.

7. Remove from heat and serve immediately, or store in the refrigerator in an airtight container for up to 2 days. Reheat before serving.

CHINESE NOODLES AND VEGETABLES IN GINGER HONEY SAUCE

Why order take-out when you can make this delicious recipe in your own kitchen?

INGREDIENTS

Serves 4

2 tablespoons coarse salt

10 cups water

1 tablespoon canola oil

1 onion, sliced very thin

1 carrot, cut into thin strips

1 tablespoon garlic, finely chopped

1 tablespoon fresh ginger, finely chopped

½ cup white cabbage, thinly sliced

½ cup fresh green beans, trimmed

1 large zucchini, cut into 2-inch-long, ¼-inch-thick strips

¼ cup honey

1 tablespoon green curry paste

1 teaspoon salt

One 8-ounce package Asian-style egg noodles, cooked according to package directions and drained

4 ounces bean sprouts

1 tablespoon soy sauce

2 tablespoons fresh basil, coarsely chopped

1 tablespoon fresh coriander

½ tablespoon red chili peppers, seeded and very finely sliced (optional)

PREPARATION

1. In a large pot over high heat, bring the salt and water to a boil.

2. In the meantime, heat a deep skillet or wok over medium heat.

3. Add the oil, onion, carrot, garlic, ginger, cabbage, green beans, and zucchini and cook for 3 minutes, stirring constantly.

4. Add the honey, curry paste, and salt and cook for 3 minutes.

5. Remove the skillet from heat and set aside.

6. Add the cooked noodles to the skillet with vegetables. Add the sprouts, soy sauce, and basil and cook over high heat for 3 minutes, stirring constantly.

7. Remove from heat and let stand for 5 minutes.

8. Transfer to serving dishes, garnish with coriander and chili peppers, and serve immediately.

HONEY-ROASTED CHICKEN THIGHS

Salty soy sauce is a perfect counterbalance for sweet honey.

INGREDIENTS

Serves 4

⅓ cup honey

2 tablespoons olive oil

3 cloves garlic, chopped

1 teaspoon salt

1 teaspoon black pepper

1 teaspoon soy sauce

4 fresh chicken thighs

1 orange, sliced into ¼-inch -thick slices

PREPARATION

1. Preheat oven to 400°F.

2. In a small bowl, mix together all the ingredients except the chicken and orange slices.

3. Place the chicken thighs in a deep baking dish, arrange the orange slices on top, and pour the sauce on top.

4. Cook for 10 minutes, then reduce heat to 375°F, and cook for 30 minutes. Serve immediately, or let cool, refrigerate for up to 1 day, and reheat before serving.

HONEY-MUSTARD SALMON FILLET

Serve this dish on a bed of pasta, roast potatoes, or steamed vegetables.

INGREDIENTS

Serves 2

2 tablespoons mustard seeds

3 tablespoons honey

1 teaspoon soy sauce

1 teaspoon white horseradish, grated

1 teaspoon salt

1 teaspoon ground white pepper

1 tablespoon olive oil

Two 8-ounce salmon fillets or steaks

PREPARATION

1. Preheat oven to 425°F. Line an 8-inch square baking pan with baking paper.

2. In a small bowl, mix together all the ingredients except the salmon.

3. Place the salmon in a prepared pan and pour over the sauce. Cook for 15 minutes. Serve immediately.

HONEY SPARERIBS

An excellent addition to a weekend BBQ. Bring this to your next one and watch them fly off the plate.

INGREDIENTS

Serves 4

⅓ cup honey

2 tablespoons soy sauce

3 cloves garlic, finely chopped

1 teaspoon dried chili flakes

1 tablespoon fresh ginger, finely grated

3 tablespoons orange juice

2 pounds pork spareribs

PREPARATION

1. In a small bowl, mix together all the ingredients except the meat.

2. Place the spareribs in a large, deep baking dish and pour over the marinade. Cover with aluminum foil and refrigerate for at least 8 hours (overnight).

3. Preheat oven to 400°F.

4. Cook the spareribs (still covered) for 30 minutes, then reduce the oven temperature to 375°F, remove the aluminum foil and cook for 30 minutes more. Serve immediately, or let cool, refrigerate up to 1 day, and reheat before serving.

Opposite: Honey-Mustard Salmon Fillet

DUCK IN POMEGRANATE HONEY MARINADE

Delicious served with steamed vegetables or white rice.

INGREDIENTS

Serves 4

2 tablespoons soy sauce

1 tablespoon fresh ginger, grated

3 tablespoons honey

2 tablespoons pomegranate concentrate

1 teaspoon black pepper

2 slices fresh duck breast, 2 inches long

PREPARATION

1. In a medium bowl, mix together all the ingredients except the duck.

2. Use a sharp knife to make slits in the duck skin.

3. Add the duck and mix well to coat. Refrigerate for 30 minutes.

4. Heat a heavy, dry skillet over high heat.

5. Add the duck to the heated skillet and cook, skin-side down, for 4 minutes. Turn and cook for 10 minutes.

6. Transfer the cooked breasts to a serving plate and cut into thin slices. Pour over skillet juices and serve immediately.

HONEY BBQ SAUCE

This delicious sauce is easy to make and perfect for both meat and chicken.

INGREDIENTS

Makes 3 cups

2 tablespoons butter

3 tablespoons chopped onion

½ cup celery, finely chopped

3 cloves garlic, chopped

3 tablespoons honey

1 tablespoon mustard seeds

2 tablespoons white vinegar

2 tablespoons brown sugar

1 tablespoon Worcester sauce

¼ cup fresh lemon juice

1 cup ketchup

½ cup bourbon

PREPARATION

1. Heat the butter in a deep skillet over high heat. Lightly sauté the onion, celery, and garlic in the skillet until golden. Mix in the honey and mustard seeds and cook for 3 minutes.

2. Mix in the remaining ingredients, reduce the heat, and cook for 10–15 minutes, or until the sauce is thick and smooth.

3. Let the sauce cool before transferring to an airtight container. Store for up to 3 days in the refrigerator.

HONEY CHICKEN BREASTS WITH ORANGE AND PINEAPPLE

Another easy way to dress up ordinary chicken breasts. You can substitute any citrus fruit for more variety.

INGREDIENTS

Serves 8

8 skinless, boneless chicken breasts

½ cup honey

4 oranges, peeled and cut into ½-inch cubes

1 cup pineapple, peeled and cut into ¼-inch cubes

¾ cup Honey BBQ Sauce (see page 92)

PREPARATION

1. Preheat the oven to 350°F.

2. Mix together all the ingredients in a large bowl.

3. Transfer to a roasting pan and cover with aluminum foil.

4. Cook for 30 minutes, remove the foil, and cook uncovered for 15 more minutes.

5. Transfer to serving plates before serving.

HONEY LAMB TAGINE WITH DRIED FRUIT

The name of this Moroccan stew is taken from the North African clay pot called a tagine, *which is traditionally what this dish is cooked in.*

INGREDIENTS

Serves 4

¼ cup honey

2 teaspoons salt

2 teaspoons black pepper

1 tablespoon olive oil

1 teaspoon cumin

2 teaspoons Spanish paprika

1 cup water

2 pounds lamb, cut into 2-inch cubes

½ cup dried apricots

½ cup prunes

½ cup dried figs

PREPARATION

1. Preheat oven to 375°F.

2. In a medium bowl, mix together the honey, salt, pepper, olive oil, cumin, paprika, and water.

3. Place the lamb and dried fruits in a ceramic casserole dish and pour over the sauce. Cover the dish and cook for 2 hours.

4. Uncover the dish and cook for 20 minutes. Serve immediately, or let cool, refrigerate for up to 2 days, and reheat before serving.

SCALLOPS IN HONEY CHILI SAUCE

Choosing fresh seafood is important. Fresh scallops should have a sweet smell and be pearly or pale golden in color.

INGREDIENTS

Serves 2

3 tablespoons honey

1 tablespoon red chili peppers, finely chopped

1 teaspoon coarse salt

1 teaspoon sesame oil

½ teaspoon lemon zest

12 medium-size scallops

1 teaspoon freshly squeezed lime juice

PREPARATION

1. In a large bowl, mix together all the ingredient except scallops and lime juice.

2. Add the scallops and mix well to coat. Refrigerate for 30 minutes

3. Heat a heavy, dry skillet over high heat. Add the scallops to the skillet and cook scallops for 6 minutes, turning once.

4. Arrange the cooked scallops on a serving dish and pour over lime juice. Serve immediately.

BUTTERED SHRIMP IN HONEY CHILI SAUCE

Choose raw, shelled shrimp that are moist and translucent, with firm flesh.

INGREDIENTS

Serves 4

¼ cup butter, softened

⅓ cup honey

2 teaspoons fresh red chili, chopped

1 teaspoon garlic, chopped

1 teaspoon ground white pepper

2 teaspoons salt

1½ pounds large shrimp, cleaned and deveined

1 tablespoon lemon juice

PREPARATION

1. In a medium bowl, mix together all the ingredients except the shrimp and lemon juice.

2. Add the shrimp and mix well to coat.

3. Place the shrimp on skewers.

4. Heat a heavy, dry skillet over high heat. Add the shrimp and cook for 3 minutes on each side. Don't overcrowd the skillet: fry the shrimp in batches if necessary.

5. Arrange the cooked shrimp on a serving platter, sprinkle with lemon juice, and serve immediately.

HONEY-BAKED FILLET OF BEEF

Serve this succulent beef with roasted potatoes to satisfy the "meat-and-potatoes man" in your family.

INGREDIENTS

Serves 4

¼ cup honey

2 tablespoons smooth Dijon mustard

1 tablespoon olive oil

2 teaspoons salt

2 teaspoons black pepper

1 teaspoon Spanish paprika

½ teaspoon nutmeg

½ teaspoon cumin

2 pounds beef or veal fillet

PREPARATION

1. Preheat oven to 450°F.

2. In a small bowl, mix together all the ingredients except the meat.

3. Place the meat on a baking sheet and rub with the spice mixture.

4. Bake for 5 minutes, then reduce heat to 400°F and bake for 10 minutes more. Let stand for 5 minutes before slicing. Serve immediately.

CALAMARI IN HONEY GARLIC SAUCE

With calamari, as with scallops, freshness is essential for healthy and tasty cooking. Look for firm, bright, off-white colored meat.

INGREDIENTS

Serves 4

3 tablespoons olive oil

1 teaspoon salt

3 cloves fresh garlic, finely chopped

1 teaspoon black pepper

2 tablespoons freshly squeezed lemon juice

½ teaspoon Spanish paprika

3 tablespoons honey

1½ pounds small calamari rings

PREPARATION

1. In a small bowl, mix together 2 tablespoons of the olive oil and ½ teaspoon of the salt with all of the garlic, pepper, lemon juice, paprika, and honey.

2. In a medium bowl, coat the calamari with the remaining olive oil and salt.

3. Heat a heavy, dry skillet over high heat. Add the calamari to the skillet and cook for 3 minutes on each side. Don't overcrowd the skillet: cook the calamari in batches if necessary.

4. Transfer the cooked calamari to a serving dish and immediately pour over the sauce. Serve immediately.

Opposite: Honey-Baked Fillet of Beef

GOOSE-WRAPPED HONEY-ROASTED CHICKEN

This divine combination of smoked goose and roast chicken will have your guests begging for more.

INGREDIENTS

Serves 4

1 tablespoon smooth Dijon mustard

3 tablespoons honey

2 teaspoons salt

2 teaspoons black pepper

1 tablespoon olive oil

1 teaspoon Spanish paprika

1 tablespoon rosemary leaves

One 4-pound whole chicken

½ pound smoked goose breast (or smoked bacon), thinly sliced

PREPARATION

1. Preheat oven to 375°F.

2. In a small bowl, mix together all the ingredients except the meat.

3. Place the chicken in a deep roasting dish, pour over the sauce, and cover with the slices of goose breast. Cook for 45 minutes.

4. Transfer the cooked chicken to a serving dish. Let stand for 10 minutes before serving, or let cool, refrigerate for up to 1 day, and reheat before serving.

HONEY-COATED SHRIMP WITH NOODLES

Using a wok to stir-fry is preferable to using a skillet since the wok is designed to distribute heat evenly and cook quickly at high heat.

INGREDIENTS

Serves 4

One 10-ounce package Chinese egg noodles

1 tablespoon soybean oil

1 tablespoon sesame oil

2 cloves garlic, finely chopped

2 teaspoons ginger, finely chopped

16 ounces shrimp, peeled and cleaned

¼ cup bamboo shoots, cut into 1-inch strips

1 carrot, cut into 1-inch strips

2 spring onions, chopped at a 45° angle

3 tablespoon honey

1 tablespoon soy sauce

PREPARATION

1. Cook the egg noodles in a large pot of rapidly boiling water until just before they are completely cooked. Drain and rinse with cold water. Set aside

2. Heat a large skillet or wok over high heat. Add the soybean oil, sesame oil, garlic, ginger, and shrimp, and stir-fry for about 2–3 minutes, or until the shrimp have changed color.

3. Add the bamboo shoots, carrot, spring onion, and cooked noodles, mix well, and cook for 1 minute.

4. Mix in the honey and soy sauce and cook for 2 more minutes.

5. Transfer to serving plates and serve hot.

HONEY-ROASTED LEMON CHICKEN BREASTS

Though the ingredients and preparation are simple, this recipe produces amazing results.

INGREDIENTS

Serves 4

1/3 cup honey

1/3 cup vegetable oil

1 tablespoon mustard seeds, crushed

1 teaspoon ground black pepper

2 teaspoons salt

1 tablespoon fresh thyme

1/3 cup fresh lemon juice

2 whole boneless chicken breasts, halved

PREPARATION

1. Preheat the oven to 400°F.

2. Whisk together all the ingredients except for the lemon juice and the chicken in a medium bowl.

3. Add the lemon juice and whisk well.

4. Arrange the chicken breasts in a high-sided pan and pour over the sauce.

5. Cover the pan with aluminum foil and cook for 20 minutes.

6. Cook uncovered for another 10 minutes or until the chicken is golden brown.

7. Serve immediately or store in the refrigerator for up to 2 days in an airtight container. Reheat before serving.

SEA BREAM FILLET IN HONEY HORSERADISH SAUCE

Sea bream may be substituted with ocean perch or red snapper in this delicate entrée.

INGREDIENTS

Serves 2

1 tablespoon white horseradish, grated

1 teaspoon garlic, finely chopped

2 tablespoons honey

1 teaspoon black pepper

1 teaspoon coarse salt

1 tablespoon olive oil

2½-pound sea bream fillets, skinned

1 tablespoon dill, chopped

PREPARATION

1. Preheat oven to 400°F. Line a baking sheet with baking paper.

2. In a small bowl, mix together all the ingredients except the fish and dill.

3. Place the fish on the prepared baking sheet, pour over the sauce, and sprinkle with dill. Cook for 12 minutes. Serve immediately.

DESSERTS AND DRINKS

HONEY YOGURT DRINK

Another drink recipe that works great with any kind of fresh fruit. Try it with papaya or guava and enjoy!

INGREDIENTS

Makes 4 cups

2 cups frozen berries

1 cup yogurt

½ cup fresh mango, chopped

3 tablespoons honey

1 tablespoon fresh mint leaves

PREPARATION

1. Place all the ingredients in a blender and blend on high until smooth.

2. Pour into tall glasses and serve immediately.

HONEY FRUIT SHAKE

You may substitute any seasonal fruit in this delicious drink.

INGREDIENTS

Makes 4 cups

1 cup frozen berries

2 fresh bananas, halved

½ cup pineapple chunks

2 tablespoons honey

1 cup freshly squeezed orange juice

PREPARATION

1. Place all the ingredients in a blender and blend on high until smooth.

2. Pour into tall glasses and serve immediately.

Opposite: Honey Yogurt Drink

FIGS WITH WARM HONEY SAUCE

Figs are among civilization's first cultivated fruits and have been used in cooking since mankind's earliest recorded history.

INGREDIENTS

Serves 2

8 large ripe figs

½ cup honey

½ cup dessert wine

1 tablespoon brandy

1 teaspoon vanilla extract

PREPARATION

1. Slice an X-shape in the top of each fig, extending almost to the bottom of the fruit (see picture). Arrange the cut figs on a serving plate.

2. In a small saucepan over low heat, bring to a boil honey and wine.

3. Remove from the heat and add the brandy and vanilla. Mix well.

4. Pour the sauce over the figs and serve immediately.

PEACHES IN HONEY SYRUP

Serve this dish topped with a scoop of gourmet vanilla ice cream or fresh whipped cream.

INGREDIENTS

Serves 4

1 cup honey

½ cup water

1 tablespoon vanilla extract

2 tablespoons fine rum

1 tablespoon lemon zest

2 large white peaches, pitted and sliced in half

PREPARATION

1. In a medium saucepan over medium heat, bring to a boil all the ingredients except the peaches. Add the peaches, reduce heat to low, cover the pan, and cook for 20 minutes.

2. Remove from heat and let cool slightly at room temperature, then refrigerate until completely cool. Transfer to a serving plate and serve chilled. Store for up to 3 days in the refrigerator.

Opposite: Figs with Warm Honey Sauce

TURKISH BAKLAVA

Baklava is a traditional Turkish delicacy that most people think must be really complicated. Try this recipe and you'll be surprised at how delicious—and easy—homemade baklava really is.

INGREDIENTS

Makes approximately 25 1½ x 1-inch rectangles

Filling:

2 cups walnuts, finely chopped

¾ cup packed brown sugar

1 teaspoon cinnamon

½ cup butter, melted

½ cup honey

Pastry:

2 pounds store-bought puff pastry

Syrup:

½ cup water

1 cup honey

1 teaspoon vanilla extract

Extra flour

PREPARATION

1. Preheat oven to 400°F.

2. Prepare the filling: In a large bowl, mix together all the ingredients until uniform. Set aside.

3. Prepare the pastry: On a floured work surface, roll out the pastry to a 24 x 30-inch rectangle, ⅛ inch thick. Cut widthwise into 2 equal portions.

4. Assemble the baklava: Place one half of the pastry on a baking sheet. Spread on half the filling. Place the second half of the pastry on top, and spread with the remaining filling.

5. Use a sharp knife to cut the baklava into 1½ x 1-inch rectangles. **Do not cut all the way to the bottom of the pastry.** (The pieces need to be connected during baking.) Cut all the way through the top layer, but only halfway into the bottom layer of pastry. Bake for 20 minutes, or until the pastry is puffy and golden brown.

6. Prepare the syrup: In a small saucepan over medium heat, bring the water and honey to a boil.

7. Remove from heat and add vanilla. Mix well and set aside.

8. When the baklava is baked, set the baking sheet on a work surface. Pour over half the syrup and brush with a pastry brush to ensure even coverage.

9. Wait for 5 minutes, then repeat with the remaining syrup. Allow baklava to cool completely before serving. Store in an airtight container at room temperature for up to 2 days.

SHEBBAKIA (MOROCCAN HONEY COOKIES)

Traditionally served during Ramadan at iftar, the evening meal that breaks the fast.

INGREDIENTS

Makes approximately 15 cookies

2 tablespoons sunflower oil

2 tablespoons water

2 tablespoons milk

2 tablespoons honey

2 cups flour

Pinch salt

Extra flour

5 cups frying oil

½ cup honey

PREPARATION

1. In the bowl of a food processor fitted with the metal blade, process the oil, water, milk, and honey until thoroughly combined. Continue to process, gradually adding flour and salt, until all the liquid is absorbed and a ball of dough is formed. Transfer the dough to a floured work surface and let stand for 30 minutes.

2. Roll out the dough to the thickness of lasagna noodles. With a sharp knife, cut into strips 10 inches long and ½ inch wide. Roll strips up (from end to end) into tight spirals.

3. In a large, deep pan or skillet, heat the oil to 360°F. Fry the spirals until golden brown. Transfer to a paper towel to drain.

4. Arrange the fried cookies on a serving plate and drizzle with honey. Serve immediately.

WHITE CHOCOLATE MOUSSE WITH HONEY-GLAZED ALMONDS

For any mousse recipe, use only the freshest eggs to avoid health risks.

INGREDIENTS

Serves 8

Glazed Almonds:

½ cup almonds, slivered

½ cup honey

¼ cup water

Mousse:

3 egg whites

¼ cup sugar

2 cups sweet cream

½ cup white chocolate, finely grated

⅔ cup honey

Butter

PREPARATION

1. Prepare the glazed almonds: Grease a baking sheet. In a medium saucepan over medium heat, cook all the ingredients, stirring constantly, until the almonds turn golden brown. Spread out on the prepared baking sheet and cool for 1 hour.

2. Set aside, or store for up to 1 week in an airtight container at room temperature.

3. Prepare the mousse: In a large bowl, beat the egg whites with an electric mixer on high speed until they begin to thicken. Gradually add the sugar; beat until the mixture forms stiff peaks.

4. In a separate bowl, whip the cream until it forms stiff peaks.

5. Gently fold the whipped cream into the egg white mixture with a spatula.

6. Melt the chocolate in a double boiler or in a bowl set atop a pan of boiling water.

7. Gently fold the melted chocolate and honey into the egg-cream mixture.

8. Divide the mousse among 8 serving bowls and refrigerate for at least 1 hour.

9. Sprinkle the chilled mousse with the glazed almond slivers and serve immediately.

FRIED HONEY SPIRALS

Frying these spirals makes them extra crispy and extra delicious!

INGREDIENTS

Makes approximately 15 spirals

2 cups water

1 tablespoon fresh yeast

2 tablespoons honey

Pinch salt

2 cups flour

6 cups frying oil

½ cup honey

PREPARATION

1. In a large bowl, mix together the water, yeast, honey, salt, and flour until smooth and doughy.

2. Wrap the dough loosely in plastic wrap and let rise in a warm place for 1–1½ hours, or until doubled in size.

3. In a large, deep pan or skillet, heat the oil to 360°F. Transfer the risen dough to a pastry bag fitted with a ¼-inch round tip. Pipe tight round spirals into the hot oil and fry until golden brown. Transfer the fried spirals to a paper towel to drain.

4. Arrange the spirals on a serving platter and drizzle with honey. Serve immediately.

HONEY MINT LEMONADE

Add a splash of bourbon for a honey-flavored variation of the traditional mint julep.

INGREDIENTS

Makes 4 cups

Juice from 4 lemons

⅔ cup honey

2 tablespoons fresh mint leaves

4 cups cold water (regular or soda)

1 cup ice cubes

PREPARATION

1. Place the lemon juice and honey in a large pitcher and mix well.

2. Add the mint leaves and cold water and mix well.

3. Add the ice cubes and serve.

Opposite: Fried Honey Spirals

HONEY-BAKED PEARS

The perfect dessert to follow a light seafood supper.

INGREDIENTS

Serves 4

6 large pears, peeled and sliced in half lengthwise

1 cup honey

½ cup water

1 teaspoon whole cloves

2 tablespoons brandy

1 tablespoon lemon zest

PREPARATION

1. Preheat the oven to 375°F.

2. Place the pears in a deep baking dish.

3. In a medium saucepan over medium heat, bring to a boil all the remaining ingredients.

4. Pour the boiling sauce over the pears and cover the dish with aluminum foil. Bake for 1 hour.

5. Uncover the dish and bake for 20 minutes. Let cool for 20 minutes, then serve immediately.

HONEY MINT POMEGRANATE DRINK

Pomegranate concentrate is available in most large grocery stores and gourmet food shops.

INGREDIENTS

Makes 4 cups

⅓ cup honey mixed with ¼ cup boiling water

1 tablespoon citrus liqueur

⅓ cup pomegranate concentrate

4 cups cold water

1 tablespoon fresh mint leaves

4 large ice cubes

PREPARATION

1. In a large pitcher, mix together the honey-water liqueur, and pomegranate concentrate.

2. Add cold water, mint leaves, and ice cubes and mix well.

3. Serve immediately.

Opposite: Honey-Baked Pears

HONEY BERRY BAKE

Best served with vanilla ice cream or fresh whipped cream.

INGREDIENTS

Serves 4

½ cup butter, chilled

¼ cup honey

1 egg

½ teaspoon salt

2 cups flour

1 pound frozen mixed berries

4 teaspoons honey

PREPARATION

1. In the bowl of a food processor fitted with a metal blade, blend together the butter and honey for 2 minutes, or until smooth. Stop the processor occasionally to scrape the sides of the bowl.

2. Stop the processor, add the egg and salt, and process for 2 minutes, until blended.

3. Stop the processor, add the flour, and process for 1 minute, or until the mixture is the consistency of breadcrumbs.

4. Preheat oven to 375°F.

5. Divide the berries evenly among 4 heatproof serving plates or individual ramekins. Spoon 1 teaspoon of honey over each dish, then cover with the crumb mixture. Bake for 15 minutes. Serve immediately.

SAFFRON HONEY PANNA COTTA

Saffron is the world's most expensive spice, but there's a good reason: it takes over 200,000 hand-harvested saffron flower stigmas to make just 1 pound of saffron spice. Thank goodness a little saffron goes a very long way!

INGREDIENTS

Serves 6

2 cups sweet cream

⅔ cup honey

½ teaspoon saffron

1 teaspoon rum

½ teaspoon granulated gelatin

3 tablespoons honey

PREPARATION

1. In a medium saucepan over low heat, bring to a boil the cream, honey, saffron, and rum, stirring occasionally.

2. Remove from heat and whisk in the gelatin, taking care to eliminate lumps.

3. Fill 6 heatproof custard cups with the hot mixture. Set aside to cool for 10 minutes at room temperature, then refrigerate for at least 3 hours until completely chilled.

4. Turn the panna cottas out of the cups onto individual serving dishes. Drizzle with honey and serve immediately.

Opposite: Saffron Honey Panna Cotta

ORANGE HONEY ZABAGLIONE

A variation on a classic Italian dessert. Serve with fresh figs to complement the zabaglione's creaminess.

INGREDIENTS

Serves 6

6 egg yolks

¾ cup honey

2 teaspoons orange zest

1 tablespoon fine citrus liqueur

1 cup whipped cream

PREPARATION

1. Place the yolks in a large bowl. With an electric mixer set to high, beat until foamy and shiny yellow.

2. Fold in the remaining ingredients with a spatula. Mix gently until thoroughly combined.

3. Transfer to serving bowls and refrigerate for at least 1 hour, or store in the refrigerator for up to 2 days.

BABA AU RHUM WITH HONEY CREAM FILLING

A French variation of the classic Baba, or "grandmother" cake, with rum to make it extra special.

INGREDIENTS

Makes 12 small cakes

Cakes:

1 tablespoon dry yeast

3 tablespoons honey

½ cup milk

4 eggs

2 cups flour

½ cup butter

½ teaspoon salt

Extra butter

Filling:

1 cup sweet cream

¼ cup honey

Syrup:

2 cups water

2 cups honey

⅓ cup dark rum

PREPARATION

1. Prepare the cakes: In a large bowl, blend together the yeast, honey, milk, and eggs with an electric mixer on medium until smooth. Add the flour, butter, and salt and mix until smooth and blended. Let rise in a warm place for 1 hour, or until doubled in size.

2. Grease 12 individual brioche pans.

3. Transfer risen batter to a pastry bag fitted with a ⅓-inch star tip. Pipe into brioche pans until half full. Let rise in a warm place for 40 minutes, or until doubled in size.

4. Preheat oven to 375°F. Bake the cakes for 25 minutes. Let cool completely in pans, then transfer all to a large baking tray.

5. Prepare the filling: In a medium bowl, whip the cream with an electric mixer on high until it forms stiff peaks. Fold in the honey with a spatula.

6. Transfer the filling to the (clean) pastry bag. Cut a short, deep "X" in the top of each pastry and pipe in a generous amount of filling.

7. Prepare the syrup: In a small saucepan over low heat, bring all the ingredients to a boil. Immediately pour over babas.

8. Serve immediately, or store for up to 2 days in the refrigerator.

SPICED HONEY ICE CREAM

Fresh vanilla pods may seem like an unnecessary ingredient, but I assure you that, for this ice cream in particular, vanilla extract does not impart a true vanilla flavor.

INGREDIENTS

Serves 8

1 ½ cups milk

½ cup sweet cream

Seeds from 1 vanilla pod

½ cup honey

½ cup sugar, divided into ¼ cups

5 egg yolks

½ teaspoon ground cinnamon

½ teaspoon ground nutmeg

½ teaspoon ground cloves

PREPARATION

1. In a large saucepan over medium heat, bring to a boil milk, cream, vanilla seeds, honey, and ¼ of a cup of sugar.

2. In a medium bowl, whisk together the remaining sugar and yolks until smooth.

3. When the milk mixture reaches boiling, reduce heat to low and carefully add the egg yolk mixture, stirring constantly.

4. Cook, stirring, until the mixture reaches 175°F. Remove from heat.

5. Pour the mixture through a fine sieve into a large bowl.

6. Add the spices and mix well.

7. Cover the bowl with plastic wrap and set aside to cool slightly, for about 10 minutes.

8. Refrigerate until completely cool, for at least 4 hours.

9. Pour the mixture into an ice cream maker and process according to manufacturer's instructions.

HONEY LEMON VERBENA TEA

If you've got a cold, this tea will make you feel a thousand times better.

INGREDIENTS

Makes 4 cups

4 cups water

¼ cup honey

3 stalks fresh lemon verbena

4 green tea bags

1 tablespoon brandy

PREPARATION

1. In a medium saucepan over high heat, bring the water, honey, lemon verbena, and tea bags to a boil. Reduce heat to low and simmer for 10 minutes.

2. Remove from heat, add the brandy, and mix well.

3. Transfer to mugs and serve immediately.

HONEY CINNAMON MILKSHAKE

Delicious as a dessert or summer treat.

INGREDIENTS

Makes 2 cups

1½ cups vanilla ice cream

⅓ cup honey

1 teaspoon cinnamon

1 cup whole milk

1 tablespoon brandy

PREPARATION

1. Place all the ingredients in a blender and blend on high until smooth.

2. Pour into tall glasses and serve immediately.

Opposite: Honey Lemon Verbena Tea

HONEY NUT TEA

Though it may seem strange, the nuts add delicious flavor—and crunch!—to this traditional North African tea.

INGREDIENTS

Makes 4 cups

4 cups water

4 bags tea (use your favorite flavor)

½ cup honey

½ cup shelled, unsalted peanuts

PREPARATION

1. Place the water and tea bags in a small saucepan and bring to a boil over low heat.

2. Remove the tea bags and add the remaining ingredients. Boil for 20 minutes.

3. Pour both the liquid and nuts into individual cups or mugs and serve immediately.

RASPBERRY HONEY INFUSION

You can use any kind of mixed berries or fruit for this delicious drink. The possibilities are endless.

INGREDIENTS

Makes 4 cups

4 cups water

½ cup dried mixed berries

¼ cup honey

1 tablespoon port

PREPARATION

1. In a medium saucepan over high heat, bring the water, berries, and honey to a boil. Reduce heat to low and simmer for 10 minutes.

2. Remove from heat, add port, and mix well.

3. Transfer to mugs and serve immediately.

Opposite: Honey Nut Tea

INDEX